HELPING OTHERS

By Steffi Cavell-Clarke

Our Values

©2017
Book Life
King's Lynn
Norfolk PE30 4LS

ISBN: 978-1-78637-065-5

Written by:
Steffi Cavell-Clarke

Edited by:
Charlie Ogden

Designed by:
Natalie Carr

A catalogue record for this book
is available from the British Library.

CONTENTS

Words that look like **this** can be found in the glossary on page 24.

WHAT ARE OUR VALUES?

Values are ideas and beliefs that help us to work and live together in a **community**. Values teach us how to behave and how we should **respect** each other and ourselves.

Respecting others

Understanding different faiths

Making your own choices

Being responsible

Our Values

Helping others

Sharing your ideas

Respecting the law

Listening to others

5

HELPING OTHERS

Many people and animals around the world need help. Everyone is able to help in one way or another, so it is important to help when we can.

There are many ways to help others. You can hold the door open for a friend, help a teacher carry their bags or help your parents around the house.

WHY IS IT IMPORTANT?

By helping each other, we can make the world a happier place.

Everyone will need help at some point in their lives. If we help others, they are likely to help us in return.

Helping someone is a kind and friendly thing to do. We should always respect and help the people that we care about.

Helping others can make you feel really good!

ASKING FOR HELP

People often need help when they have hurt themselves or feel unwell. It is important that we always ask for help when we need it.

If you ever need help, ask a responsible adult.

Kayleigh fell over when she was playing in the garden. She hurt her knee and asked her mum for help. Kayleigh's mum cleaned her cut and gave Kayleigh a hug, which made Kayleigh feel a lot better.

PEOPLE WHO HELP US

There are people who live in our community whose job it is to keep us safe. Police officers, firefighters, doctors and nurses are able to help us in an **emergency**.

Nurse

Police Officer

Doctor

Firefighter

You can help these people by acting responsibly and staying safe. It is very important that we help to keep each other safe too. You can help your friends by telling them when you think that they are doing something that is unsafe.

LISTENING TO OTHERS

It is important to listen to other people. Listening to other people can help you to understand what they are thinking and feeling.

Sarah listened to her friend Jack when he told her that he finds it difficult to open the classroom door. She wanted to help him, so now Sarah always holds the door open for Jack.

HELPING OTHERS AT SCHOOL

It is important that we help others at school. We can help the teacher by being quiet when they are talking. This will also help other children in the class to be able to hear what the teacher is saying.

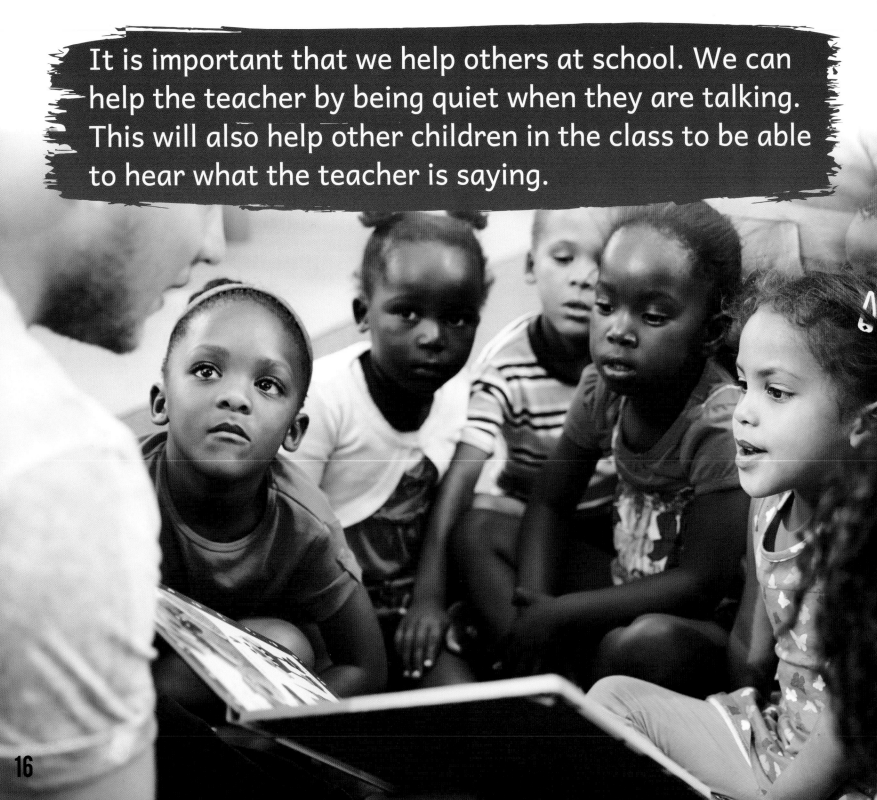

Teachers help us to learn new things at school. They teach us maths, science and how to read and write.

Helping your teacher will make their day easier.

HELPING OTHERS AT HOME

Parents often work very hard to care for their family. You can make their day easier by offering to help.

If you would like to help but don't know how to do something, just ask!

There are often lots of jobs to do around the house, such as cleaning and tidying. Matt tidies his bedroom to help his mum. He also sets the table for dinner while his dad is cooking.

HELPING THE ENVIRONMENT

We can help our community by helping the **environment**. We can do this by throwing our rubbish in a rubbish bin and **reusing** plastic shopping bags.

Reusing our rubbish is called recycling. We can recycle many things, such as paper, cardboard and plastic. Recycling helps to keep our environment clean.

MAKING A DIFFERENCE

Parents often love it when you take time out of your day to help them. Try to help them today!

Help with the shopping.

Help carry the bags.

Hold the door open.

Keep your bedroom tidy.

Set the table.

Even though it is nice to help others, you still need to keep yourself safe. Remember to always tell a parent or **guardian** before speaking to or helping a stranger.

23

GLOSSARY

community	a group of people living in the same area who share similar values
emergency	a dangerous problem that requires action straight away
environment	nature or the natural world
guardian	a person who looks after something or someone
law	the rules that a community has to follow
respect	feeling that something or someone is important
responsible	to be trusted to do the right thing
reusing	using something again or more than once

INDEX

PHOTOCREDITS